COACHING QUARTERBACK PASSING MECHANICS

Steve Axman

COACHES CHOICE

ISBN: 1-57167-194-3
Library of Congress Catalog Card Number: 97-69613

Book Design: Mariah L. Oxford and Michelle A. Summers
Cover Design: Deborah M. Bellaire
Cover Photos: Sean Oppenshaw
Interior Photos: Bill Pegram

Coaches Choice Books is a division of: Sagamore Publishing, Inc.
                                          P.O. Box 647
                                          Champaign, IL 61824-0647
                                          Web Site: http//www.sagamorepub.com

To my mentor, Coach Homer Smith

ACKNOWLEDGMENTS

I certainly consider myself a student of the game and, as a result, feel very fortunate to have had some great teachers. No person has had a greater influence upon me in my efforts to write such a book as *101 Quarterback Drills* and on my own coaching than my dedicatee, Coach Homer Smith. I had the great fortune of having been able to work under Homer for three years at the United States Military Academy at West Point. Homer taught me what offensive design and structure was all about, how to apply "geometry" football coaching and how to coach technique with precision. Although our philosophies may have taken slightly different roads, Homer Smith's teachings are deeply embedded in almost all of my football thinking. Homer's greatest gist was that he, indeed, truly made me think.

Although I only spent one season working for Mouse Davis with the Denver Gold in the USFL, I certainly was able to learn much while with him. And, although they may not realize it, I have benefited greatly from studying such great quarterback coaches as Lindy Infante, Paul Hackett, and Sam Wyche.

CONTENTS

Football is a great game I have been fortunate enough to coach for almost three decades. During that period of time, I have had the opportunity to observe and work with quarterbacks at all levels of competitive play—high school, intercollegiate and professional. In each instance, the importance of the quarterback being able to consistently exhibit sound passing mechanics has been reinforced countless times.

I wrote this book because of my perception that a need exists for coaches at all competitive levels to be aware of what constitutes sound quarterback passing mechanics and what steps can be undertaken to teach those mechanics in an appropriate manner. To enhance the effectiveness of *Coaching Quarterback Passing Mechanics* as a productive teaching tool, the information presented in this book has been divided into seven chapters: "pre-snap stance," "receiving the snap," "dropping back to pass," "setting the snap," "delivering the pass," "sprint-out passing," and "passing mechanics drill teaching progression." To the extent possible, I have attempted to present the information in a straightforward, step-by-step detailed manner.

Hopefully, this book will serve as a sound blueprint for teaching, developing, and refining quarterback passing mechanics. To the extent that it accomplishes that objective, it will have achieved its primary purpose.

CHAPTER 1

Pre-Snap Stance

The passing quarterback must start with a good pre-snap stance to enable him to best read the fronts and coverages facing him. A good pre-snap stance also will enable the quarterback to begin his drop-back stepping action efficiently without false stepping.

The quarterback places his feet at shoulder width, which is a fairly narrow, or bunched, stance. Too wide of a stance is a major cause of false stepping, an action that the quarterback must avoid. A right-handed quarterback staggers his left foot backwards approximately six inches in a toe-to-instep relationship. Such a slight stagger actually helps put the quarterback six inches deeper into his drop. More importantly, the slight stagger action of the feet helps to eliminate false stepping action of the left foot when the quarterback starts with even foot positioning. From an even alignment of his feet, the quarterback often (whether he is thinking about it or not) takes a short punch step forward with the left foot so that he can push off his left foot more comfortably to get into his drop-back action. Such a forward punch step by the left foot will actually shorten the quarterback's drop. In addition, the left-foot punch step is often the reason (along with too wide of a stance) that a quarterback is stepped on by his center, an action which can cause the quarterback to be tripped up. The quarterback must, however, be sure that his stagger is consistent. He cannot stagger the left foot for certain actions and the right foot on others. This action would only produce keys for the defense. The slight left foot stance stagger for a right-handed quarterback is shown in Diagram 1-1.

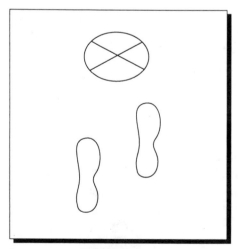

Diagram 1-1: Slight left-foot stance stagger for a right-handed quarterback.

The quarterback's toes can be turned in slightly in an effort to create a "digging in" action of the inside cleats. This position will best enable good pushing off action as the quarterback works into his drop. The heels of the quarterback's feet rest on the ground lightly. Such action enables the majority of the quarterback's body weight to be on the balls of his feet, helping to eliminate flat-footedness.

The quarterback bends at his knees to position his hands underneath the center and to create an athletic carriage of his body. He *does not* bend at his waist to place his hands underneath the center. Bending at the waist produces flat-footedness, locked out, stiff leg positioning and a dropping action of the head. Such a dropping of the head cuts back on downfield visioning ability. The quarterback stands tall with his chin up and chest out to best enable him to vision the defense. Any hunched over, or rounded back, action cuts down on that vision ability. Proper pre-snap stance action is shown in Figures 1-1 and 1-2.

Figure 1-1: Pre-snap stance—frontal view.

Figure 1-2: Pre-snap stance—lateral view.

Finally, the quarterback wants to position himself closely enough to the center to allow for a slight amount of comfortable arm bend at the elbows. Such arm bend action allows the quarterback to ride the center's movement consistently with his hands as he starts into his drop-back action until the center's snap of the football breaks the quarterback's hands apart. If the quarterback positions himself too far from the center, he will force himself to lock out his arms at the elbows, producing straight arm positioning. When the quarterback has locked out, (i.e., straight) arms, he will not have the ability to ride the center's movement as he begins his drop-back action which often leads to quarterback-center exchange miscues. Proper and improper alignment and arm bend for the quarterback when under the center are shown in Figures 1-3 and 1-4.

PROPER AND IMPROPER ALIGNMENT AND ARM BEND WHEN UNDER CENTER

Figure 1-3: Properly bent arms.

Figure 1-4: Improperly locked-out, straight arms.

PRE-SNAP SHOTGUN STANCE

A shotgun quarterback's pre-snap stance aligns at five and a half to six yards, depending on the offer's preference of depth. The quarterback's feet are shoulder-width apart. However, his feet are placed even to one another to best allow the quarterback to step to the left or right. The knees must have a degree of flexion. The quarterback does not want to be lock-legged and, as a result, flat-footed. The quarterback must have such an athletic carriage of his body so that he may act like a baseball shortstop in regard to any type of poorly snapped football from the center.

Once the shotgun quarterback is ready to receive the snap (after any line-blocking calls or wide-receiver adjustment calls are made), the quarterback extends his hands out to the center. The palms must face down with good, but comfortable, finger spread. This address of the football, with the extended hands, can actually act as the signal to the center that the quarterback is ready for the snap whether the snap count is silent (on the center's discretion) or via the quarterback's verbal cadence. At this point, the shotgun quarterback must be sure to lock his eyes on the football in the center's hand(s) in case of a miscue and an early snap by the center. The shotgun quarterback's stance is shown in Figure 1-5.

Figure 1-5: The quarterback's shotgun stance.

CHAPTER 2

Receiving the Snap

When receiving the snap from the center, precise and consistent hand positioning is the initial key. The top right throwing hand (for a right-handed quarterback) is placed firmly up under the center's rump. The fingers of the top hand are well spread to press up against as much of the center's pant cloth as possible. The palm of the top hand faces down, parallel to the ground. The middle finger of the top hand is placed directly down the seam of the center's pants. The thumb of the top hand is spread out in such a manner as to be nearly parallel to the line of scrimmage. Proper top hand placement by the quarterback under the center's rump is shown in Figure 2-1.

Figure 2-1: The quarterback's top hand placement under the center's rump.

The quarterback's bottom hand is placed in a position that allows the thumbs of both of his hands to mesh comfortably. The knuckles offset so that the bottom hand is slightly behind, or under, the top hand. This position allows for the fat of the hand, underneath the thumb, to address the football. If the knuckles offset so that the bottom hand is slightly in front of, or over, the top hand, then too much "air" will address the football from underneath the heels of both hands. Such "air" can be a major reason for a center-quarterback exchange miscue and a resultant fumble. The proper hand positioning thumb mesh is shown in Diagram 2-1.

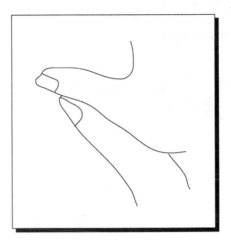

Diagram 2-1. The quarterback's hand position—thumb mesh.

The bottom hand is the hand that actually places the upward pressure of both of the quarterback's hands up under the center's rump. Good bottom hand pressure helps to guarantee constant pressure of both hands up under the center's rump as both the quarterback and center begin their stepping actions. In other words, placing pressure with the bottom hand allows the quarterback to ride the center with both hands. Conversely, if the quarterback's hand pressure is placed with the top hand, the quarterback will be more apt to ride the center's movement with the top hand only, causing a natural breakage of the two hands as they separate. Such breakage, or separation, often becomes another major reason for center-quarterback exchange miscue and resultant fumbles. Proper two-handed and improper one-handed riding action of the center is shown in Figures 2-2 and 2-3.

PROPER TWO-HANDED AND IMPROPER ONE-HANDED RIDE OF THE CENTER

Figure 2-2: Proper two-handed ride (pressure with bottom hand).

Figure 2-3: Improper one-handed top hand ride.

In a proper snap action by the center, the football breaks the heels of the quarterback's hands, thereby forcing the fingers of the quarterback's hands to envelop the ball naturally. The fingers of the right, throwing hand should receive the laces of the football in such a manner that the football is ready to be thrown with a minimum of adjustment.

After the football is placed in the quarterback's hands via the center's snapping action, the football is immediately drawn to the quarterback's stomach, or "third hand." Such action helps to secure the football immediately so that it is safe from any hand or arm slapping action by either an offensive lineman or a defensive player. Proper securing of the football to the "third hand" stomach area after receiving the snap from the center is shown in Figure 2-4.

Figure 2-4: Securing the football to the third-hand stomach area.

RECEIVING THE SHOTGUN SNAP

The key to receiving the shotgun snap is to have the quarterback lock in his focus and maintain his level of concentration. Once the quarterback raises his hands to address the snap of the football from the center, his eyes *must* be locked on the football. Such action will help eliminate the possibility of a miscue if the center were to mistakenly snap the ball early. The shotgun quarterback must actually see the ball begin to move with the coordinated shotgun snap action of the center's hand(s). He then must actually see the football leave the center's snap hand(s). He then must follow the flight of the snapped football *all the way to his own hands!* He must concentrate so intently that he tries to see the contact of the football with his fingers. The shotgun quarterback should catch the ball with his fingers (not his palms) so that he can best gain control of the football immediately. Once the shotgun quarterback looks the ball into his hands, he *then* looks up to study the coverage and/or prime routes of his receivers.

CHAPTER 3

Dropping Back to Pass

Getting maximum depth on all drop-back actions by the quarterback is a must. Such maximum drop depth aids the blocking scheme in design because the defensive rush will have a further distance to go to get to the quarterback. In addition, deepened drops give the quarterback more time to read his keys and possibly allow him to step up into the pocket if an intense defensive rush occurs from the outside.

INITIAL DROP-BACK STEP

When dropping back, the quarterback's initial concentration is on the stepping action of the first initial depth step. The quarterback's first step is for as much depth as possible with the toe pointing to almost a 180° turn. The radical step angle helps to open up the quarterback's hips properly in his effort to "get away" from the line of scrimmage. The initial (close to 180° angle) turn step is shown in Diagram 3-1.

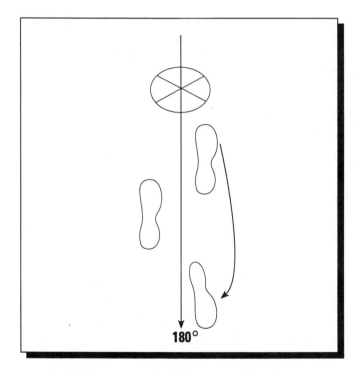

Diagram 3-1: Quarterback's close to 180° initial drop-back step.

A body lean of an approximate 60° tilt from the ground (or 30° tilt from perpendicular to the ground) is now of utmost importance. Some coaches refer to this as back, or right, shoulder drop (for the right-handed quarterback) in an effort to produce such lean. Such an approximate 60° angle tilt of the body helps to ensure a proper depth of step away from the line of scrimmage as shown in Figure 3-1.

Figure 3-1: Sixty-degree angle tilt of the quarterback's body on his first initial drop step.

STEPPING FOR DEPTH

On five- and seven-step drops, a formula is used. The last two steps (to be discussed later) are a cross-over throttle step and a plant step to bring the dropping quarterback back under control and to allow him to set-up. Thus, on a five-step drop, the first three steps are steps for depth with the 60° angle body tilt or lean. The last two steps are cross-over throttle and back foot plant steps. On a seven-step drop, the first five steps are steps for depth with 60° angle body tilt or lean. The last two steps, again, are cross-over throttle and back foot plant steps. Whether it is three- or five-depth steps, all effort is made to take as deep a depth step or depth cross-over step as possible with the assistance of the approximate 60° angle tilt, or lean, of the body. Again, a dropped back right shoulder (for a right-handed quarterback) is another way of saying 60° angle body tilt or lean. The five- and seven-step drop-back actions are shown in Diagram 3-2.

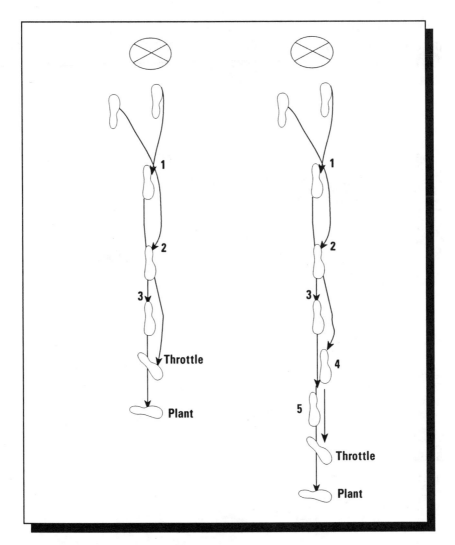

Diagram 3-2: Five- and seven-step drop-back action.

Lack of body tilt, or lean, during the taking of the depth steps produces an action called "prancing." When prancing, the quarterback's body remains perpendicular to the ground as his knees and legs work straight up and down during the dropping back for depth stepping action. Such action produces shortened steps and, as a result, a shortened drop.

Many coaches feel, and teach, that whether or not the drop is five or seven steps, the third step is the step that "opens up" the drop-back stepping action and allows for the greatest distance of all the steps. Some coaches actually teach the third step as a special skip action type step in which the quarterback actually reaches back as deep as possible to help gain the greatest amount of distance from the line of scrimmage.

During the depth steps, the quarterback should rock the ball tightly across his sternum or upper-belly area. The elbows should be kept in tightly to the body as well to ensure a tightly gathered, efficient dropping action. Elbows that are out away from the body during the rocking action tend to produce a floppy, shortened

60° ANGLE TILT AND ROCK ACTION ON DROP

Figure 3-2: First step.

Figure 3-3: Second step.

Figure 3-4: Third step.

drop. In addition, the quarterback must be sure to *not* cock the football up in a pre-pass throwing position during the dropping back for depth stepping action as this will only hinder the quarterback's effort to set up with proper depth. Figures 3-2, 3-3, and 3-4 show proper three-step drop-back action with a proper 60° angle body tilt and a tightly efficient rocking action of the ball across the sternum or top of the belly.

STEPPING TO SET UP

The last two steps of a five- or seven-step drop, as illustrated in Diagram 3-2, are a cross-over throttle step and a back foot plant step. On the next to the last cross-over throttle step (after the three or five steps for depth at the 60° angle tilt or lean have been taken), the quarterback brings his body back under control by shortening the next-to-last cross-over step. The quarterback now brings his body back up to a perpendicular-to-the-ground position. The final plant step brings the quarterback to a full, upright controlled passing stance. Figures 3-5 and 3-6 show the last two cross-over throttle and back foot plant steps that put the quarterback in his controlled passing stance. The desired depth from the line of scrimmage on a five-step drop should be from six and one half to seven yards. A seven-step drop should provide the quarterback with an approximate depth of eight to nine yards.

LAST TWO STEPS TO PUT THE QUARTERBACK IN CONTROLLED PASSING STANCE

Figure 3-5: Next-to-last cross-over throttle step.

Figure 3-6: Last back foot plant step.

THREE-STEP DROP

Three-step drop action is a bit different. Because the three-step drop will not allow much depth of drop by design, a slight modification is made in the second, cross-over step to produce as maximum a depth as possible. On a three-step drop, the quarterback takes his normal first, or initial, close to 180° angle turn step in his effort to "get away" from the line of scrimmage. On the second, cross-over step, however, the quarterback utilizes an elongated skip-type step in an effort to add even just a few extra inches before taking his third plant step. On the average, the second elongated skip-step type action can help to produce six to eight extra inches of depth to the three-step drop. Any extra amount of depth, even if it is only inches, can be of utmost importance to the three-step drop action. The problem with three-step drop-passing action is that the quarterback sets up much closer to the line of scrimmage and, as a result, the offensive line. Since the shortened dropped quarterback must still throw over the top of the blocks of his offensive linemen and the rush of the defense, any increased depth, even inches, can be extremely helpful. The second, elongated cross-over skip-step action of the three-step drop is shown in Diagram 3-3.

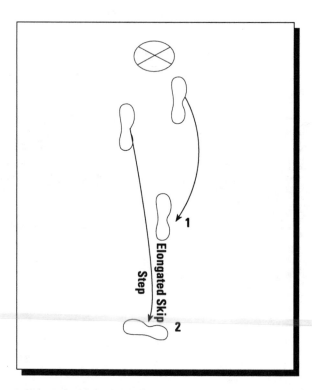

Diagram 3-3: Second, elongated cross-over skip step on three-step drop.

TWO-STEP DROP

Two-step drop action is a specialized drop-back action set used to throw the fade route on the goal line when inside the five-yard line. Being so close to the goal line, the quarterback doesn't have time to take a normal three-step drop. In essence, the quarterback takes one drop step with his right foot (for a right-handed quarterback). The single plant, drop step must angle the quarterback's hips right or left towards the direction of the throw. When throwing to the left, the drop plant step is backwards and slightly to the left. The second step by the left foot is merely a slide step to help the quarterback balance his body for his pre-pass stance to deliver the quick fade pass. The two-step drop action to deliver the close-in goal line area fade throw is shown to the left and right (right for a right-handed quarterback) in Diagram 3-4.

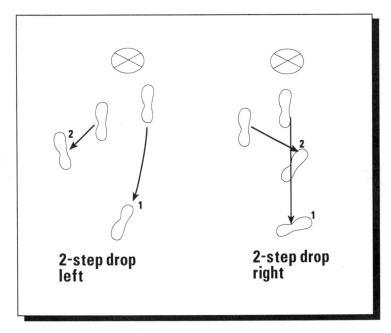

Diagram 3-4: Two-step drop.

CHEATED STEPPING FOR SIDELINE THROWS

For highly-timed passes thrown to the left (for a right-handed quarterback), the quarterback utilizes "cheat steps" on his last two throttle, plant steps to enable his hips and body to be set to the left, thereby ready to make an immediate sideline throw. A major throwing problem can occur when a right-handed quarterback sets up with a positioning for a pass to be thrown straight down field when, in essence, he actually is going to make a sideline throw to the left. With his hips and body set for a straight ahead down-field throw, the right-handed quarterback is forced to swing his front left foot, his hips, and his body trunk to the left to make the left sideline throw. As a result, the natural body torque and swing of the body to the left can pull the thrown football down and away to the left. To accurately deliver the pass, the quarterback must actually add extra arm power to the delivery to get the football to go where he wants it to go.

To rectify this problem, the quarterback utilizes cheated cross-over throttle and plant steps to set-up with his body actually facing towards the left sideline pass target point. Such a cheated set-up will now allow the quarterback to properly step at his pass target without having to swing his body with the resultant natural pull of the thrown football down and to the left.

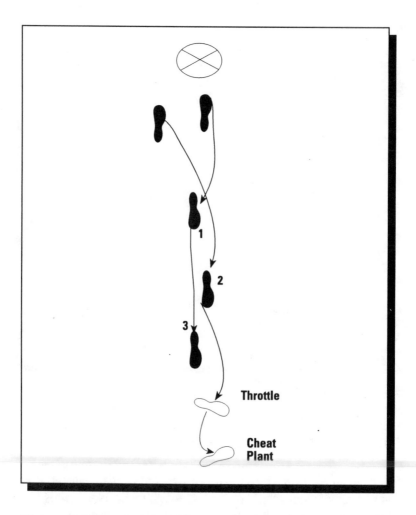

Diagram 3-5: Cheated last two cross-over throttle and plant steps to open a right-handed quarterback's hips to the left.

To have his stance properly turned and set to the left, the quarterback does not fully cross-over his next-to-last throttle step backwards. Instead, he steps slightly forward towards the right sideline on the cross-over throttle step. On the last plant step, the quarterback swings his right, back foot around to the right to turn his hips, and body to the left as he sets. The cheated, last two throttle, plant steps for a five-step drop are shown in Diagram 3-5. The action is no different for a three- or seven-step drop since all of the cheated set-up stepping action takes place on the last two cross-over throttle and back foot plant steps.

SHOTGUN DROP-BACK ACTION

The shotgun drop-back action takes on a slightly different action than the normal three-, five- or seven-step drop. However, a difference also exists between three-step shotgun drop timed action and five- or seven-step shotgun drop-timed action.

On three-step shotgun drop-timed action, the quarterback, once he has looked the ball into his hands, simply "pops-up" in place, turning his hips left, center or right to align with his pass target spot. Since the pass action is only three-step timed, he will not have any extra time to drop back further. The time that is taken to get the football back to the quarterback via the center's shotgun snap action eats up the time needed to be in sync with the quick, three-step timed throw action. Shotgun three-step timed, "popping up in place," setting action is shown in Figures 3-7 and 3-8.

SHOTGUN THREE-STEP TIMED DROP-BACK ACTION

Figure 3-7: Receiving the snap.

Figure 3-8: Popping up in place.

On a five- or seven-step timed throw action, the shotgun quarterback actually takes a short three-step drop after receiving the snap to put him at an approximate depth of seven to nine yards. The shotgun quarterback's first step is, once again, for depth. However, he doesn't need to take a radically deep first step as he does when he starts from under the center for he has already given himself the advantage of the shotgun alignment depth. In addition, he doesn't have to worry about the approximate 60° angle tilt of the body or the back shoulder drop action for the same reason. The shotgun quarterback simply looks the ball into his hands, takes an approximate 180° angle depth step, and then utilizes his last two cross-over throttle and back foot plant steps to set up. The shotgun quarterback's last two cross-over throttle and plant steps are the same as on normal drop-back action from underneath the center. As a result, the quarterback is able to get into his normal flow of drop back set-up steps for at least the last three steps of his drop. This helps to now set up a comfortable and similar flow into the actual pass delivery stepping action. Cheated throttle/plant step considerations must also be taken into account. Five- and seven-step timed shotgun drop-back action is shown in Figures 3-9 to 3-12.

SHOTGUN FIVE- AND SEVEN-STEP TIMED DROP-BACK ACTION

Figure 3-9: Receiving the snap.

Figure 3-10: Initial step for depth.

Figure 3-11: Cross-over throttle step.　　**Figure 3-12: Back foot plant step.**

As has been stated, five- and seven-step timed throw action utilizes the same three-step drop action by the quarterback after he receives the snap even though the route timings may be different. Seven to nine yards is plenty of depth from the line of scrimmage whether the route depth timing is for a five- or seven-step timed throw. Any deeper than nine yards will produce overdropping. Overdropping is when a drop-back quarterback, whether from a shotgun formation or from under the center, drops to depths of ten yards or more from the line of scrimmage. Although deep drops allow for the potential to step up in the pocket when pressured from the outside, overdropping is the action that can make it impossible for the offensive tackle to position himself in a defensive end's rush lane. Overdropping can simply put the quarterback so deep that all the offensive tackle can do is to wheel out to the outside and push the end-of-line rusher out wide with his hands since the defender is too wide for the offensive tackle to position his body in front of. Diagram 3-6 shows the geometry of the overdrop problem.

BACKING OUT DROP-BACK ACTION

Straight, backing out drop-back action is not used as widely as it once was. However, it still does have merit—especially if the offensive passing system utilizes quick "hot" type dump passing to backs and tight ends. Since the quarterback keeps

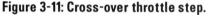

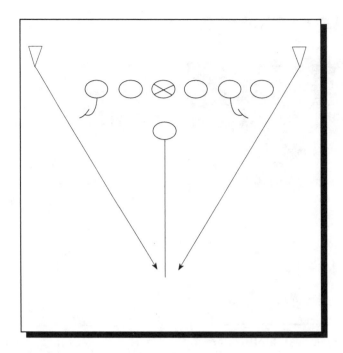

Diagram 3-6: Overdropping produces rush lane angles too difficult for offensive tackles to block.

his shoulders square to the line of scrimmage on the first four or six steps of the straight, back-out drop-back action, he is in a much better position to see and throw such quick dump passes both to the left and right. The downside to straight, back-out drop-back action is that it involves a slower drop-back action and doesn't lead to the quarterback getting as much depth from the line of scrimmage as possible. With the blitz-oriented, pressure defenses currently popular in football, slower drop-back action and lessened depth are definitely not an advantage.

In the straight, back-out drop-back action, the quarterback initially steps straight back with his right front foot (due to the slight stagger of the left foot). He then simply continues to step straight back for the next three or five steps depending on whether or not the drop-back action is for a five-step timed throw or a seven-step timed throw. Although the quarterback cannot get the 60° angle tilt lean that was previously pointed out as an integral element of regular drop-back action, the quarterback still needs to lean back to help get as much depth as possible. In addition, the straight, back-out drop-action quarterback must be sure to carry the ball just under his chin and rock the ball from side to side across the top of his chest as he takes his straight, backing-out steps. Such a high carriage of the football will allow the backing-out quarterback to be able to dump pass the football quickly with a quick release. If the backing out quarterback were to rock the ball across his belly, he would slow the speed of release ability down tremendously. He would now have the added time of having to draw the ball up to his chin before he can even begin his actual pass-action delivery of the football. Figures 3-13 and 3-14 illustrate the initial straight, backing-out drop-back action.

INITIAL STRAIGHT, BACKING-OUT DROP-BACK STEPPING ACTION

Figure 3-13: Backing out lean.

Figure 3-14: Football rocked across the top of the quarterback's chest.

On pure, straight, back-out drop-back action, the quarterback simply pivots on his fourth left-footed step if it is a five-step timed pass. If it is a seven-step timed pass, the quarterback pivots on his sixth, left-footed step. Much like the cross-over throttle step of a normal drop back, on the pivot step, the quarterback brings himself under control by getting out of his backward lean and getting to a more perpendicular positioning to the ground. Cheated plant step considerations for the last plant step must be taken into account. Diagram 3-7 shows the straight, back out drop-back action for a five- and seven-step drop.

A commonly used straight, back-out drop-back action is to combine straight, back-out drop-back action for the first four steps with a normal turned three-step drop-back action throttle/plant step finish. Such action is used for the deeper seven-step timed throws but allows the quarterback the advantages of straight, back-out drop-back action for the first four steps for quick, dump type passing. This stepping action is shown in Diagram 3-8.

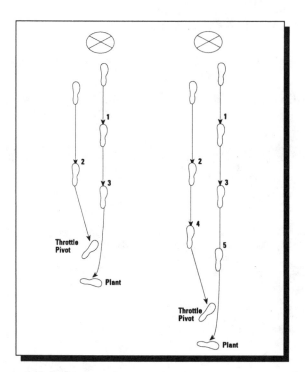

Diagram 3-7: Five-and seven-step straight, back-out drop-back action.

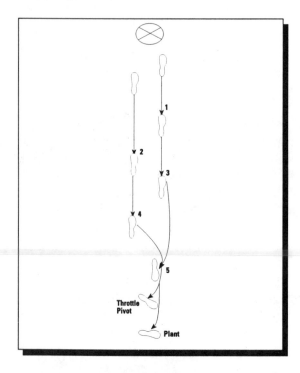

Diagram 3-8: Combined straight, backing out and normal seven-step drop-back action.

MOVE-OUT DROP-BACK ACTION

Move-out drop-back action is a type of drop-back action in which the quarterback moves out to the left or right to set up in an area just inside of or directly over the tackle. It is a drop-back action that helps to move the quarterback's launch point so that the defensive rush is not able to lock in on one specific drop-back launch point behind the center. Also, the quarterback is moving away from the backside of the rush. In addition, move-out passing can help a quarterback with a long throw to the field from a hashmark by shortening the distance of the throw slightly and by providing a more favorable throw angle. The only drawback to move-out drop-back action is that the quarterback cannot get as much depth from the line of scrimmage as he does on normal, straight drop-back action due to the geometrical angle taken to move out to the wider launch point.

The move-out drop-back action takes on the same action as a normal five- or seven-step drop-back action (for a right-handed quarterback going to the right) with the exception of the angle of approach taken to the launch point behind the tackle. The first three steps on a five-step move-out drop, or, the first five steps on a seven-step move-out drop are depth steps toward the desired launch point spot. The last two steps, whether it is for a five- or seven-step move-out drop, are, again, throttle/plant steps.

For a right-handed quarterback going to his left, a slightly different action is utilized. The right-handed quarterback will now take five steps to the left launch point (on a five-step move-out drop) and then pivot back to the inside, swinging his right foot backwards to set-up. Once again, a hopping around action to the inside can be utilized once the fifth step hits the ground to set up. On a seven-step move-out drop to the left for a right-handed quarterback, the pivot (or hop) action would simply be made off the seventh, left-footed step. As a result, the five- and seven-step move-out drop-back actions to the left for a right-handed quarterback add a sixth and eighth step, respectively, with the pivot, or hop, action. Diagram 3-9 shows move-out drop-back action to the left and right with a five- and seven-step drop depth.

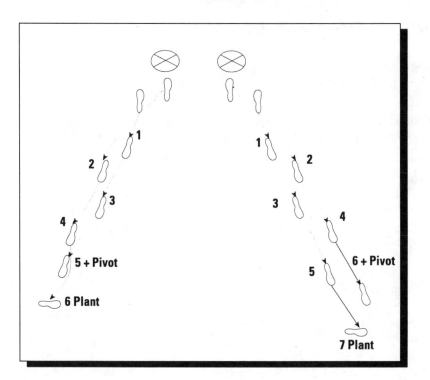

(5-step move-out drop-back action left) *(5-step move-out drop-back action right)*

Diagram 3-9: Five- and seven-step move-out drop-back action left and right.

CHAPTER 4

Setting Up to Pass

GRIPPING THE FOOTBALL

It is very important for the quarterback to grip the football comfortably with his fingers, his thumb and the heal of his hand. Where a quarterback grips the football in relation to further back, more towards the tip, or closer up towards the center, fat of the football depends on the size of the quarterback's hand. The smaller the quarterback's hand, the more he must grip the football more towards the ball's tip. The larger his hand, the more the quarterback can grip the football towards the middle, fat part of the ball. One way or the other, at least one of the quarterback's fingers should rest across the laces to help provide control. The proper grip of the football is shown in Figure 4-1 and 4-2.

THE PROPER GRIP OF THE FOOTBALL

Figure 4-1.

Figure 4-2 .

The football should not be "palmed" (an action in which the palm of the hand is in contact with the football in a pressing fashion). There must be "air" between the football and the palm of the quarterback's hand. In addition the index finger of the throwing hand must not be too far from the rear tip of the football. Both actions, palming and an index finger too far from the tip of the football, will lead to a hard, nose-down passed football that is hard to catch. Figures 4-3 and 4-4 illustrate both proper and improper gripping of the football with regard to palming.

PROPER AND IMPROPER GRIPPING OF THE FOOTBALL IN REGARD TO PALMING

Figure 4-3: An improperly gripped, palmed football.

Figure 4-4: A properly gripped football with "air."

PASSING STANCE

When the quarterback hits his final drop-back plant step, he should be in an upright position with a slight knee bend. Locked out legs produces flat-footedness. The slight knee bend allows for an athletic carriage of the body. The upper torso should be leaning forward, out towards the sideline with a slight bend at the waist. The quarterback should feel the weight of his upper body over the balls of his feet to help produce an athletic passing stance.

The quarterback's feet should be approximately shoulder width apart. It is better to have his feet too close together in the stance than spread too far apart. This tight, or bunched, stance best helps to accommodate proper pass delivery stepping action. Slightly more weight is distributed on the back foot in the passing stance to help accommodate a pushing off action off the back foot as the quarterback transfers his weight to his front foot in the pass delivery stepping action.

The football should be held with two hands. The two-handed hold of the football helps to ensure ball security as well as to help produce a firmly gathered upper body. The hold of the football is somewhere in the vicinity of the upper back breast or back collar bone (note: every quarterback can be somewhat different in the actual carriage of the football since it is important for the quarterback to feel comfortable). In this way, the football has a minimum distance to be drawn backwards before the pass delivery motion is executed. The football should not, however, be held so closely to the body so as to restrict the pass delivery motion of the arm in any way. In addition, the ball should not be held low, near the belt level, because such action slows down the actual delivery of the pass since the football has to be drawn back further to fully cock the football. Many coaches accuse their quarterbacks of having slow releases when, in essence, these quarterbacks are simply holding the football too low when in their passing stance—an action which necessitates a longer, slower, draw of the football to get to a fully cocked position. Some coaches feel that the proper hold of the football in the passing stance should be in front of the sternum. This author, however, feels that such a hold of the football naturally drops the upper-body throwing platform (the shoulders and tops of the upper arms). A low carriage of the upper body throwing platform can lead to a slower release, a lower release and a pass that has the tendency to take-off too high.

Besides the high hold of the football in the passing stance, the quarterback must be sure that his back shoulder is drawn back fully (i.e., or fully cocked) so that his back shoulder does not have to be drawn back any further to deliver the pass. A back shoulder that is not fully cocked, or worse, shoulders that actually face towards the line of scrimmage, are other reasons that a quarterback can have a slow delivery. Few quarterbacks actually have a slow delivery. More often that not, they simply have a low carriage of the ball and/or a back shoulder that is not fully cocked.

In addition to a high hold of the football, the quarterback must concentrate on a high, somewhat level throwing platform. The throwing platform consists of the tops of the shoulders and the tops of the arms. To get such a high, level throwing platform, the quarterback lifts his elbows. Lifting the front elbow is a fairly natural action for the quarterback. It is the back elbow that most quarterbacks want to tuck in tight to their side. Such a tucked in, dropped back elbow produces an unwanted tilt of the throwing platform and shifts the majority of the quarterback's body weight in the passing stance to his back foot. Although it is desirable to have slightly more weight distributed on the quarterback's back foot to accommodate a push off action off the back foot to begin the actual pass delivery motion, the majority of the weight should not be placed on his back foot. As will be fully discussed in Chapter 5, back-foot throwing, which starts with the majority of the body weight resting on the back foot in the passing stance, disallows proper body torque and transference of the quarterback's body weight to his front foot during the actual pass delivery motion. The importance of keeping the back elbow up in the passing stance to help produce a fairly balanced passing stance with a high, level throwing platform cannot be emphasized enough. Figures 4-5 and 4-6 show a proper passing stance.

A PROPER PASS DELIVERY STANCE

Figure 4-5.   Figure 4-6.

READING WITH THE FEET

Most pass plays are designed to have the quarterback set-up in his passing stance (be it three-, five-, or seven-step drop or move action), plant his back foot and immediately begin his front foot stepping to start the actual pass delivery to his prime pass route target (as will be discussed in Chapter 5). However, where passing to the prime route may be the ideal thought, the reality may be that the quarterback is forced to pass the football to the second, third, fourth, or even fifth receiver read as he goes through the progression of the pattern read's design.

What is important in such a read progression is that the quarterback reads *with his feet*, not just his eyes. As the quarterback goes through this read progression from receiver to receiver, he must reset his feet to each potential receiver just as his eyes move, or scan, to those secondary receivers. By reading with his feet (resetting his feet to each new receiver), the quarterback allows himself to immediately be ready to step at each new target to deliver the pass if that particular receiver is open. By not reading with, or resetting, his feet to each new potential pass target receiver, the quarterback will actually form an improper setting of the feet away from the actual pass target spot. As a result, the quarterback may end up delivering a pass with an improper set of his feet to the desired target spot. Proper reading with the feet action is shown in Figures 4-7 to 4-11.

READING WITH THE FEET STANCE RESETTING ACTION

Figure 4-7: Read #1.

Figure 4-8: Read #2.

Figure 4-9: Read #3.

Figure 4-10: Read #4.

Figure 4-11: Read #5.

SHUFFLE (RE)SETTING

There are some passing systems that will have the quarterback set up for a five-step timed throw with a five-step drop and then have the quarterback take two additional drop steps for added depth to throw to a seven-step timed outlet route. This action is called shuffle setting or, more correctly, shuffle resetting.

From a set stance (after the five-step drop action has been taken), the quarterback simply takes two more steps for depth with an additional cross-over/plant step action. Using a cross-over step as the initial shuffle (re)set allows the second step to be the plant step, thereby, enabling the quarterback to now step with the front foot to throw immediately. Some coaches prefer to shuffle (re)set by stepping with the back foot first with a subsequent slide back action of the front foot before another slide-back plant-action step of the back foot. This second shuffle (re)set action, however, is much slower. The recommended cross-over/plant shuffle (re)set action is shown Diagram 4-1.

An important consideration in the shuffle (re)set action—and the phase where a quarterback can easily break down in fundamentals—is that the quarterback *must* get back to a proper passing stance once he shuffle (re)sets. Such resetting action must see the quarterback get back to proper passing stance fundamentals. The breakdowns that often occur involve having the quarterback reset to a lock-legged, flat-footed stance and/or hold the football low in its carriage. The chance of success of executing a well-thrown pass from such a poor pre-pass stance is, as a result, greatly diminished.

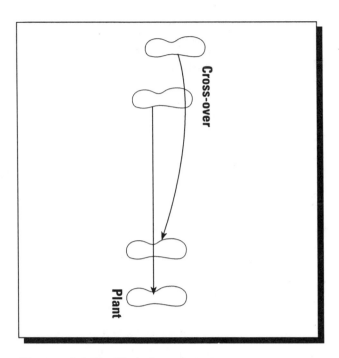

Diagram 4-1: Shuffle (re)set action.

SCRAMBLE RESETTING

Much like the shuffle (re)set action, being forced to reset due to evasion of defensive rush can easily lead to a breakdown of passing stance fundamentals. If a coach were to do a breakdown analysis of successful passes in relation to primary or secondary sets, he would quickly find that his quarterback's best passes are from his initial, or primary, set up. Unless the pass rush is on top of the quarterback immediately, the quarterback gets his best chance to set up properly in a good passing stance on his initial drop. It is when the quarterback is forced to reset his passing stance due to pass rush evasion that the coach will usually see the quarterback's pass competition percentage plummet. Why? Because the quarterback is now forced to reset quickly, under continued pass rush duress.

In other words, he simply may not have the time to reset to a proper passing stance. A poorer stance correlates to poorer pass delivery mechanics. This is why with football's current emphasis on pressure defense, the slow-footed quarterback is having trouble succeeding. A quick, nimble-footed quarterback is better able to avoid such a pass rush and reset quickly into a proper pass delivery stance. Much like the shuffle (re)set action, resetting with a lock-legged, flat-footed stance and/or a lower hold of the football usually leads to a breakdown in pass delivery efficiency. It would be much like a golfer scrambling three or four yards to his left or right and quickly trying to hit a golf ball effectively without having the time to reform a proper stance. Similar to the fact that a golfer would have substantial problems hitting a good golf shot without a good stance, a quarterback would, likewise, have trouble effectively delivering a good pass from a poor pre-pass stance.

If the quarterback is flushed from his primary set a few feet to his right or left, the quarterback simply releases his front, security hand from the football to allow his arms the freedom to assist the forward or backward stepping, or running, action of the feet and legs. If a right-handed quarterback has to bail out to his right four or five yards or more, the quarterback will actually run to the new set-up point in his pass rush evasion attempt. The quarterback must also be ready to duck under a jumping pass rusher stepping up into the pocket. On all of the pass rush evasion actions, the key is for the quarterback to reset into this secondary set-up action with a proper passing stance. He must have a proper knee bend to allow for an athletic stance. The football must be brought back up to a high carriage position. Resetting to a proper passing stance is of paramount importance to delivering a well thrown pass from such a secondary set-up.

When a right-handed quarterback is forced to bail out to his left four or five yards or more, he must turn *away* from the line of scrimmage, initially, he must turn towards the opposite end zone in an effort to run around a hard rushing end from his back, and often, blind vision side. If he were to turn to the inside towards the line of scrimmage when bailing out to the left, he might run directly into the path of a hard rushing backside defensive end who is hard for the quarterback to see. Diagram 4-2 shows the bail-out course of a scrambling right-handed quarterback to his left.

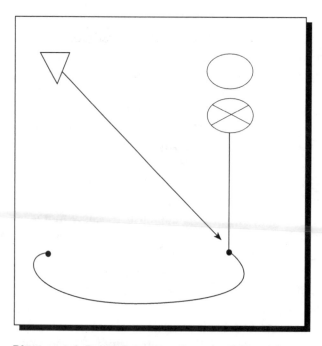

Diagram 4-2: Bail-out course of a scrambling right-handed quarterback to his left.

Once a right-handed quarterback bails out to his left and arrives at his secondary set-up spot, he must spin around to reset-up in a proper passing stance. He must again ensure tht he has proper knee bend in order to have an athletic carriage of his body as well as a high hold of the football.

CHAPTER 5

Delivering the Pass

BACKWARD DRAW OF FOOTBALL

From the passing stance, with a fully cocked back shoulder, the quarterback draws the football back to a fully drawn position. It is extremely important for the throwing elbow to also be drawn back and up so that the throwing arm works to a postion parallel to the ground. Such arm positioning will vary from quarterback to quarterback since it is important that they feel comfortable. The shoulder and throwing arm positioning from a parallel-to-the-ground alignment (level throwing platform) can vary according to the desired height trajectory of the pass—a factor that will be discussed later in this chapter. The higher the desired height of the pass, the greater will be the tilt of the throwing platform (shoulders and tops of arms) from a parallel to the ground position. However, no matter what the trajectory of the pass, the quarterback must avoid a body positioning, or stance, in which the throwing elbow is tucked in tightly to the body. A tightly tucked in throwing elbow leads to back foot throwing. Such action produces poor body torque in relation to the transferring of the quarterback's body weight from his back foot to his front step foot during the actual delivery of the pass.

During the drawing back action of the football to its furthest, backward point, the wrist of the throwing hand must be kept firm and straight, but not rigidly locked. Such a firm hold of the wrist will help to produce a tight spiral spin of the passed football. When the football is drawn back, the front nose of the football will face backwards. However, the quarterback wants to maintain the firm hold of the football by not breaking his wrist when the football is drawn to its furthest point. A break in the wrist means that the wrist will have to be firmed up again as the quarterback begins his forward throwing motion. Such a readjustment of the wrist can put unwanted extra play in the release action of the pass producing a wobble action of the football in its flight. Figure 5-1 shows the proper action of drawing the football back to its furthest point before the forward passing motion begins.

FRONT FOOT DIRECTION STEP

The forward motion of the actual pass delivery begins with a coordinated lead of the free elbow, the arm and the hand and the forward stepping action of the front

Figure 5-1: Fully drawn backward position of the football.

foot. The front elbow and the front step foot extend out directly to the target spot (the actual delivery point) of the pass. It is important for the quarterback to realize that this target spot may be directly at a receiver who has stopped or who is coming directly back to the quarterback on his route execution. In addition, the target spot may be to a point where the line of the pass will intersect the path of a receiving who is crossing the field horizontally and/or diagonally. The step foot actually steps just beyond the target spot (just to the left if a right-handed quarterback). Such a slight over-step allows for a comfortable swing-through action of the hips to the target spot. If the quarterback steps directly at the target spot, a greater chance exists for a less fluid rotation of the hips towards the target spot. In essence, the stepping action of the front foot and the swing-through action of the hips fight one another rather than allowing for a comfortable mesh of the step and hip swing actions if the front foot direction step is directly at the target spot on the pass.

If the quarterback oversteps too far to the left of the target spot (for a right-handed quarterback), he will end up having to use extra throwing arm follow through to get the passed football to go where he wants it to. The overstepping action to the left will have the effect of pulling his body to the left, thereby forcing him to have to compensate with his arm and hand follow through. What is now happening is that the stepping action and the pass release action are not working together in harmony. If the right-handed quarterback understeps to the target spot to his right, he will, again, find his hip rotation action fighting through his understepping action which will drastically affect a smooth pass delivery. Proper, short, front foot stepping action is shown in Figure 5-2.

Figure 5-2: Front foot stepping.

As was previously mentioned, the front step is not a big step. Although each quarterback's front step may differ in length due to variances in individual physical leg length, it must be short enough to force the upper torso to actually roll, or fall, over the ball of his planted front foot. Too big a front step forces his upper torso to position its weight towards his back foot with a subsequent break of the body at the hips. In essence, the hips and lower body are left behind as the upper torso snaps forward from the hips. Such action has the effect of either a release that is too high, thereby forcing the football to take off high on the quarterback, or a situation where the football is pulled down low with substantial loss of pass delivery torque and power. Straight-legged stepping, often associated both with

Figure 5-3: Improper straight-legged overstepping.

overstepping and tall quarterbacks, also produces the same negative pass-action results. Figure 5-3 shows improper, straight-legged overstepping of the front step foot that results in a situation where the quarterback is forced to snap his upper torso forward from his hips.

POP-UP/HITCH-UP STEPS

On most five- and seven-step timed throws, the quarterback does not hit his back fifth- or seventh-plant step and immediately step and throw. He might on a very quickly timed five-step timed pass. More often than not, the quarterback will hit his fifth, or seventh-plant step and will utilize two, quick, short, pop-up, gather type steps with his front and his back feet to begin the actual pass-delivery action. As mentioned previously, these steps are, simply, two short, quick, gather steps that both help give time to gather the upper torso body parts and help create a step timing action to better fit in with the timing delivery of the pass to the particular route being thrown to. The front foot pop-up step is approximately six to eight inches. The back foot pop-up step simply steps up to match the front foot pop-up step to help regather the throwing set-up base before the front foot pass delivery step is taken. Figures 5-4 to 5-7 shows the pop-up pass-delivery stepping action.

Figure 5-4: Plant step.

Figure 5-5: Front pop-up step.

Figure 5-6: Back foot gather to reform base.

Figure 5-7: Front foot pass delivery step.

Hitching-up is a similar, but differently executed concept both in technique and in focus. On passes to deeper timed routes, such as a hook/curl route or a streak route, the quarterback can help both his timing and his forward, torque stepping power by hitching-up. The term "hitching-up" means that after the quarterback hits his fifth- or seventh-plant step, he steps up into the pocket with a deliberate twelve-to-fourteen inch hitch-up step with both his front delivery step foot and with his body. The action is much more than a pop-up to gather step. Instead, the quarterback is taking a significantly bigger step to help propel his entire body forward as if to provide a powerful jump-start for the actual front foot delivery step. The quarterback takes the front foot hitch-up step, matches that step with a similar back-foot step to regather the throwing set-up base before executing the front foot delivery step. Such action helps to provide extra torque body power into the continuous stepping action of the pass delivery. The only major concern about the use of hitch-up stepping is that there may not be enough room between the quarterback and the offensive line to hitch-up step into if the pass rush is backing the offensive linemen into the face of the quarterback. In this case, the quarterback is forced to only pop-up step into the pocket before delivering the pass. Hitch-up stepping action is shown in Figures 5-8 to 5-11.

HITCH-UP STEPPING

Figure 5-8: Plant step.   Figure 5-9: Front hitch-up step.

Figure 5-10: Back foot gather to reform base.

Figure 5-11: Front foot pass delivery step.

USING THE CHEST

The passed football is actually directed to its target spot with three body-part actions. The first, front foot directional stepping, has already been discussed. Directing the passed football with the chest is the second. The third, arm, hand and finger follow-through action, will be discussed later in this chapter.

By utilizing the chest to direct the football, two vital concepts are achieved. First, using the chest to direct the passed football helps to properly direct all parts of the body trunk from the hips to the belly to the chest in a straight line direction to the target spot. Second, by driving the passed football with the chest, the quarterback will help to provide maximum body torque and power in the delivery of the pass. In addition, directing and driving the pass with the chest helps to transfer the body weight of the quarterback from his back foot to over the ball of his front foot delivery step. The quarterback, from a high, level throwing platform, emphasizes the drive of the football by sticking out and directing an expanded chest cavity at the pass delivery target spot. Such action helps to produce a coordinated, continuous movement with the stepping out of the forward, front foot, the whipping action of the hips, and the power, drive directional action of the chest. Some coaches place a major emphasis on the coaching of the whipping hip action in the pass delivery. This author feels that when a quarterback concentrates on the whipping hip action of the pass delivery, he stands the chance of leaving his chest behind and not getting the maximal advantage of his chest with regard to nice, tight upper body torque power. By concentrating on the use of his chest to both provide direction and body torque power, the quarterback will automatically produce proper hip whipping action.

The drive of the passed football with the chest to provide maximum body torque and resultant power to the delivery of the pass cannot be over-emphasized: Each quarterback has only so much arm strength in relation to the power of his pass delivery. Extra power in a pass can only be added via the torque of the body torso led by the drive action of the chest. There are times when a quarterback must "finesse" a pass with "touch". And yet, he still may need a desired amount of power to get the pass to the target spot with proper authority. By driving the passed football with the chest, the torque of the body's forward motion can provide such needed pass power while the arm, hand and index finger of the throwing arm puts the desired finesse "touch" on the pass delivery. Figure 5-12 highlights the use of the chest to provide pass delivery direction and maximal body torque power.

Figure 5-12: Using the chest to direct and drive the pass.

OVERHEAD DELIVERY

The actual delivery of the pass is a desired overhead (i.e., over the top of the ear) delivery much like a baseball catcher's peg to second base. Most quarterbacks will feel substantially more comfortable with a plane less than directly overhead. However, the emphasis should still be on as high an overhead release as possible to assist a full range of the throwing motion. In addition, the higher the release point of the football in the passing motion, the greater the ability of the quarterback to throw the football over the rush of the defense. The height of the quarterback can certainly be a major factor in aiding a desired high release. However, if a tall quarterback throws with a side arm motion and/or a motion that is across his chest, he will simply have a relatively tough time getting the desired trajectory on the pass, as well as getting the pass over the top of the defensive rush. The height of the quarterback is not necessarily the most important ingredient to a successful release. The height of the release point of the overhead, over-the-top-of-the-ear pass delivery is. Figure 5-13 shows the proper overhead, high release delivery action.

Figure 5-13: Overhead high release delivery action.

FOLLOW THROUGH

It was previously mentioned how the passed football is directed by three body part actions. The first two were the front foot directional step and the directional drive action of the chest. The third is the follow through action of the passing arm, hand and index finger.

During the actual pass delivery, the throwing wrist must be kept firm and straight (but not locked) to help produce a tight spiral spin on the ball. A breaking action of the wrist as the football leaves the hand and the index finger will put extra play in the football's spin thereby causing wobbling action. Instead, the quarterback must maintain the firm hold of the wrist throughout the release action as his thumb rotates downward to help produce a natural, screw-ball type spiral rotation of the football. The football is released with an actual snapping action of the wrist and a full extension (i.e., lock-out action) of the elbow to help provide the desired amount of velocity.

Many coaches teach that as part of the pass delivery follow-through action, the quarterback should rotate the thumb of his passing hand down to his left pocket (for a right-handed quarterback) to produce proper rotation follow through. This author does not feel that such a thumb-to-pocket relationship is always correct. For example, if a quarterback throws a pass straight ahead, the thumb-to-pocket follow-through action should naturally happen. However, not all passes are thrown directly in front of the quarterback. Radical throws to the left and right, especially when the quarterback cannot fully reset his feet as he may want, can produce a pass delivery action in which it would be unnatural for the thumb to rotate down to the left pocket. As a result, this author feels that is much more important to emphasize a natural, rotation of the thumb in a downward fashion to help create the desired screwball type rotation of the passed football. Such an action may, or may not, be to the left pocket.

Index finger follow through to the target spot is the final body part that is an integral factor (the first two being the front foot direction step and the driving lead of the chest) in directing the passed football. The index finger, the last body part that touches the football in the passing action, is pointed directly at the target spot. If a pass is thrown high, it is usually because the index finger is pointed high. If the pass is thrown low, too far to the left, or too far to the right, it is usually because that is the point at which the index finger is pointing. Pointing, however, is not necessarily the best of terms to use because the quarterback does not want to freeze his index finger to actually point at the target spot of the pass. Instead, the index finger directs the pass to the desired target spot and falls through naturally with the downward rotation of the thumb.

The desired sequence of directing the pass is now complete. The quarterback begins with proper front foot direction stepping. He then drives the pass with his chest (helping to provide desired torque power and direction) at the target spot. He then follows through with his throwing arm, his hand and, especially, his index finger to complete the direction of the passed football. A proper coordination of all three of these body parts helps to efficiently allow the body to deliver the passed football to the target spot without distraction and with maximal body torque power. Such a coordinated sync allows for a tight, accurate spiral to be thrown where the quarterback wants it to be thrown. Figures 5-14 and 5-15 illustrate proper follow-through action.

PROPER FOLLOW THROUGH

Figure 5-14: Index finger direction of the football.

Figure 5-15: Downward rotation of the thumb on the follow through.

BACK OUT FOLLOW THROUGH

When using a back-out drop, an extra finger (index finger) follow through must be utilized to direct the passed football to the target spot. Most often employed on quick dump, crossing or hot type passing, the quarterback must realize that the backward lean of his back-out drop action wants to naturally pull the throwing arm, the hand and the index finger downward. Such a natural, downward pull action will most often result in a low thrown pass. The quarterback must understand this problem and correct it by emphasizing a high release of the football in the pass delivery action and an extra finger follow through of the index finger to the target spot of the pass. The quarterback still wants to rotate his thumb downward to help produce the desired screwball-type rotation of the passed football. However, in this case, the quarterback actually should freeze action (i.e., point his index finger at the target spot of the pass to overcompensate for the body's natural pulling down action of the delivery arm and hand due to the back-out drop action). Proper back-out drop extra finger follow through action is illustrated in Figure 5-16.

Figure 5-16: Extra finger follow through on back-out drop action.

TRAJECTORY PASSING

The lone exception to a high, level throwing platform with the back elbow up in preparation for the pass delivery involves a situation when the quarterback wants to put high trajectory on the passed football in an effort to drop the passed football into a target spot with the nose of the football down. Whether a quick fade route throw to the corner of the end zone or a deep, streak throw down the field, the quarterback must change his throwing platform to produce the desired high trajectory of the pass.

If someone wanted to use a cannon to try to lob or drop in a shell, the task would involve raising the angle of the cannon and the gun sight to produce the desired angle of the flight of the shell. Likewise, the quarterback must raise his gun sight (i.e., his front shoulder) by tilting his level throwing platform backwards. The back, throwing elbow now drops downward toward the quarterback's trunk. However, the quarterback still does not want to tuck his throwing elbow tightly to his body. The majority of his body weight is now definitely shifted to his back foot. However, the quarterback definitely does not want to back-foot throw (i.e., throw with the majority of the body weight remaining positioned on the back foot). Back-foot throwing will produce a pass that dies when it reaches its zenith (highest) point due to the fact that the front nose of the football remains upward as the football descends. As a result, the fat of the football is what breaks through the air as the football descends, thereby causing loss of power and the dying action of an underthrown pass.

The proper pass delivery of a football in which high trajectory is desired is to direct all three pass delivery body parts at the zenith point of the pass. Although the raising of the shoulder gun sight and dropping of the back shoulder and level throwing platform produces a sitting action on the back foot in the set-up stance, proper high-trajectory pass action now shifts to the front directional step foot just as on any other type of pass. The difference is that the quarterback directional steps at, leads with the chest to and follows through with throwing arm, hand and index finger to the zenith point. Such action properly shifts the body weight, torque and power to the front directional step foot. Following through to the zenith point of the high-trajectory pass allows for the passed football to "turn-over" so that the front nose of the football is what breaks through the air as the football descends. Such a nose-down football allows for the proper aerodynamics of the football to take place. The football will now be able to cut through the air with a minimal amount of loss of power and allow the football to drop to its target spot with proper force. Diagram 5-1 shows the desired "turn-over" action of the passed football as a result of proper follow through to the zenith point of the pass. It also shows a nose-up football that dies as a result of back-foot throwing and improper follow through to the zenith point of the pass. Figures 5-17 to 5-20 illustrate proper trajectory pass delivery action.

On quick, one- or two-step corner-of-the-end-zone fade route throws, the quarterback will probably not have the time or the space in front of him to step at the zenith point of the high-trajectory pass. However, the lead of this chest and his throwing arm, hand and index finger follow-through action must all be directed to the zenith point of the quickly thrown fade route to help produce the desired turn over of a nose-down passed football after it reaches its zenith point.

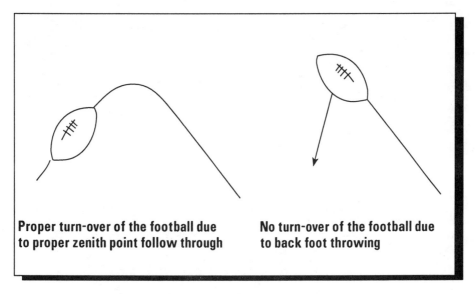

Proper turn-over of the football due to proper zenith point follow through

No turn-over of the football due to back foot throwing

Diagram 5-1: Turned over and non-turned over trajectory pass as a result of proper or improper follow through to zenith point.

Figure 5-17: Back foot, high-trajectory tilt of pass set-up.

Figure 5-18: Front foot stepping at the zenith point.

Figure 5-19: Follow through to the zenith point.

Figure 5-20: Natural thumb down follow through rotation.

CHAPTER 6

Sprint-Out Passing

Sprint-out passing is part of the family of the move-out passing that was discussed in Chapter 3 that there is a definite move of the quarterback's launch point from where he will throw his pass. However, unlike the set-up move launch point somewhere over the playside offensive tackle, sprint-out passing has the quarterback passing while on the move. The advantages of sprint-out passing are twofold. First, the launch point is moved, thereby helping to keep the defensive rush off balance and helping the sprint-out quarterback to run away from the back-side half of the rush. Second, the quarterback, in his sprint-out attack of both the perimeter and the line of scrimmage, becomes another threat that the defense must cover. If the defense brings up a perimeter defender to stop the quarterback's run threat, one less defender can be used in the defensive pass coverage. If the defense floods the pass coverage with a maximum amount of coverage defenders and ignores the sprint-out quarterback, the quarterback now becomes an effective run threat to the defense.

An additional advantage to sprint-out passing involves the usage of an athletic quarterback who runs well. Sprint-out passing can act much like the threat of run-option action, in which the quarterback becomes an extra offensive threat to defend as a result of his run option threat. On sprint-out passing, an athletic sprint-out quarterback who is a good runner, threatening both the perimeter and the line of scrimmage, presents the defense with a threat it cannot ignore.

Another advantage to the use of sprint-out passing lies in the aid it gives to a short quarterback. By sprinting the short quarterback to the outside, he is put in a position out on the perimeter in which the defensive front's rush is not directly in front of him. This scenario enhances his ability to view the coverage in front of him as well as see the execution of the routes of his receivers.

Disadvantages to sprint-out passing are three-fold. The first lies in the fact that, by design, the backside of the field gets cut off from the quarterback with regard to him being able to effectively throw to the backside of the field. Second, the defense is able to rotate its coverage with the quarterback's run sprint-out action and to effectively provide extra coverage defenders to flood the area in front of the sprint-out quarterback. Third, a sprint-out quarterback is much more vulnerable to the physical rush pressure of the defense, since he has no longer has his offensive line in front of him to protect him. Once he decides to tuck the ball under his arm and run, he becomes a ballcarrier.

SPRINT-OUT STEPPING

The initial steps of sprint-out passing are similar to the stepping actions of setting up for the move-out launch point. The quarterback will step out to a point that represents the desired depth and width of the sprint-out action. This desired point can vary substantially depending on the actual design philosophy of the sprint-out offense utilized and with regard to the step timing of the quarterback's throw and the receivers' routes. The author will utilize a depth and width of directly behind the tackle on the sprint-out action before he begins to step up to throw for his example.

On a five-step timed sprint-out drop for a right-handed quarterback going to the right, the quarterback takes three steps for depth at the sprint-out point behind the tackle. Just as in normal drop-back action, the sprint-out quarterback looks to get as much depth as possible. The fourth step begins the sprint out turning-up action back towards the line of scrimmage. This action is called the "flattened up" step because the sprint-out quarterback starts stepping back up into the line of scrimmage. On the fourth, flattened-up step, the toe of the left foot must be turned back up into the line of scrimmage just slightly passed a parallel plane to the line of scrimmage. Such a "flattened-up" step, slightly into the line of scrimmage, helps to turn the hips and the body of the running quarterback back towards the line of scrimmage.

The final, fifth step of a five-step sprint-out action for a right-handed quarterback going right is the actual step that the sprint-out pass is made over. The fifth, right-footed step is taken directly at the target spot of the pass. The quarterback's body now rolls over his right foot as the sprint-out pass is delivered. Follow through then naturally falls through to the next, left-footed sixth step. Diagram 6-1 shows five-step sprint-out action for a right-handed quarterback going to his right.

Five-step sprint-out action for a right-handed quarterback going to his left actually becomes a six-step sprint-out action. One extra step is needed for the right-handed quarterback going to his left to allow for the left-footed, "flattened up" step with the left foot slightly up into the line of scrimmage. Such action allows for the final, sixth delivery step of the right foot to step directly at the target spot as his body rolls over his right foot to deliver the sprint-out pass. Similar to five-step sprint-out action to the right, follow through then naturally falls to the next, left-footed step. Diagram 6-2 shows the extra step action on five-step, timed sprint-out pass action to the left for a right-handed quarterback.

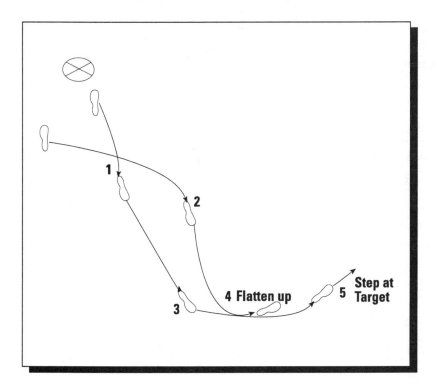

Diagram 6-1: Five-step sprint-out drop for a right-handed quarterback.

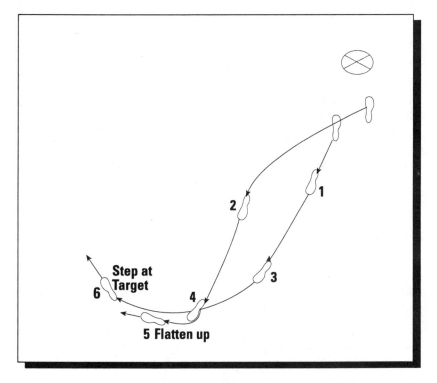

Diagram 6-2: Extra step on five-step timed sprint-out action to the left for a right-handed quarterback.

Seven-step, timed sprint-out action (that times out with routes by the receivers more in the eighteen-yard stem range) simply adds two more steps to the depth-stepping aspect of the sprint-out action regardless of whether the quarterback is going to his right or left. Of course, if the right-handed quarterback sprints out to the left on seven-step, timed sprint-out passing, an extra, eighth step is added to allow the right-handed quarterback to execute a "flatten up" step with his left foot and a delivery step with his right foot at the target spot. Diagram 6-3 shows seven-step, timed sprint-out stepping action to the left for a right-handed quarterback.

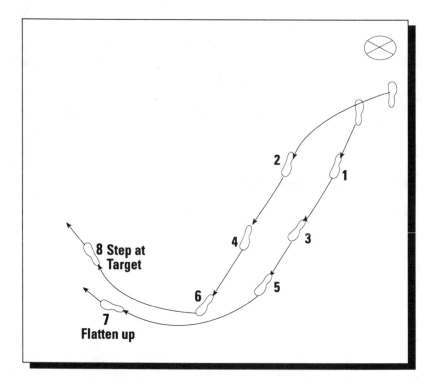

Diagram 6-3: Extra step in seven-step, sprint-out action left for a right-handed quarterback.

SPRINT-OUT PASS DELIVERY

All throughout the depth stepping of the sprint-out action (from three to six steps depending on whether the right-handed quarterback is going to his left or right), the quarterback rocks the ball back and forth across the top of his belly to help assist in the depth-stepping action. The sprint-out pass-delivery action begins on the left foot "flatten up" step, which helps the sprint-out quarterback to begin turning his hips and shoulders towards the pass target spot. The important point to be emphasized is that the sprint-out quarterback must divorce his upper-torso throwing action from his lower-body run action during the actual sprint-out pass-delivery action. This focal point is not as easy as it might seem because the running action naturally wants to detract from sprint-out pass-delivery action of the upper body.

As the right-handed quarterback steps up with his right-delivery step foot, the quarterback must draw the ball up and across his chest to cock the football in a normal, high-level throwing-platform position. Although the chest is now directed at the pass-delivery target spot, the football must still be drawn to its normal high hold position somewhere off the top of the quarterback's back (right) shoulder. A proper sprint-out passing cock of the football is shown in Figure 6-1.

Figure 6-1: Proper sprint-out cock of football.

Emphasis should now be placed on driving and leading the ball with the chest to help provide both power and direction, an overhead delivery and proper hand/index finger follow through. Coming over the top with the sprint-out pass delivery and with index finger follow through cannot be overemphasized. Typically, the lower run action wants to detract from the quarterback's sprint-out overhead release and force him to throw in a more of a sidearm fashion. This situation must be totally avoided because sidearmed sprint-out throwing will blend in with the running action of the lower body to provide extra play in the sprint-out pass release. Getting the ball up in the sprint-out pass-delivery set-up and drive leading the passed football with the chest helps to efficiently gather the entire body for effective sprint-out pass action.

Extra finger follow through (involving the index finger) on the sprint-out pass-delivery action is of utmost importance. Similar to the backout drop-pass delivery action, the body wants to naturally pull the pass down and to the left (for a right handed quarterback) on sprint-out action due to the running action of the lower body. As a result, extra index finger follow through to the target spot of the pass is crucial. The term extra finger follow through means that the quarterback actually freezes, or points the index finger of his passing hand at the target spot as he releases the pass. The thumb of the throwing hand still rotates downward to help produce the desired screwball-type rotation of the football. Eventually, the throwing arm and hand will follow through down and across the body as the quarterback takes his natural, next left-footed step. However, the actual sprint-out pass delivery is made over the right, direction step made to the target spot of the delivery. The upper torso rolls over the right, direction step foot. The quarterback drives the football with his chest, executes an overhead delivery and applies extra index finger follow through action. Figures 6-2 to 6-4 illustrate a proper sprint-out pass-delivery action.

SPRINT-OUT PASS DELIVERY ACTION

Figure 6-2: Sprint-out cock of the football.

Figure 6-3: Overhead sprint-out release.

Figure 6-4: Extra sprint-out finger follow through.

Poor sprint-out pass-delivery action is usually the result of a continued low carriage of the football as the quarterback starts to take his forward, right-foot delivery step at the pass target spot. Such action will usually produce a pass that releases on the rise, taking off high on the quarterback. In addition, the lack of extra index finger follow through will often pull the pass down and to the left (for a right-handed quarterback).

One final concern involving sprint-out passing is the lack of stepping up at the pass target point via the "flatten up" step with the next-to-last left-foot step and a continuous right-foot pass-delivery step at the pass target spot. Instead, the sprint-out quarterback continues his last two steps towards the sideline. This action will force the right-handed sprint-out quarterback to throw across his body when sprinting out to the right as his body actually fights the sprint-out throwing action since his body's movement is directed towards the sideline. When sprinting out and to the left, the opposite problem occurs for a right-handed quarterback if his last two steps are towards the sideline. Such action will force the quarterback to throw a sprint-out pass behind his body action, usually in a sidearm fashion. The "flatten up" step which helps turn the hips and shoulders up into the line of scrimmage and the last, right-foot direction step at the pass target spot help to eliminate such problems. However, when sprinting out to the left, the right-handed quarterback must place extra emphasis on properly cocking the football over his right shoulder.

CHAPTER 7

Passing Mechanics Drill Teaching Progression

The final chapter of *Coaching Quarterback Passing Mechanics* presents a drill teaching progression of 10 passing skills drills to specifically help teach, coach and practice the quarterback passing mechanics skills presented in the first six chapters of this book. The drills begin with the practice of the most basic of the passing mechanic skills. The drills then sequentially progress to help coach, teach and practice more specific passing skill need off of a variety of pass-set actions that a quarterback may specifically deliver the pass from. The drills progress from stationary passing mechanic drills to drills integrating the total pass action of the pass set-up and subsequent pass action. For a more complete reference of quarterback passing mechanic drills coaches should refer to *101 Quarterback Drills**.

Whatever drill a coach utilizes, he must understand that any drill used must, in itself, have a specific goal or purpose in the development of his quarterback. A drill is not just busy work to fill up assigned individual practice time on the practice schedule. Instead, the coach must utilize his drills as teaching and coaching tools to practice specific skill development needs for his quarterback. A drill creates the opportunity for a coach to teach specific skills, reinforce correct performance and correct improper performance of the skills. Drills allow for quarterbacks to learn and hone their passing mechanics through predetermined practice repetitions. Repetitions of correct performance is the key. Positive reinforcement and corrections made in easy-to-fix verbiage and tone help to ensure progress towards consistently correct performance. A lackadaisical, get-through-the-period attitude by the quarterback or the coach *cannot* be allowed. Individual drill time and the subsequent drills used to help develop a quarterback's passing mechanics must be well planned, goal oriented and efficiently coached and administered on a daily, weekly and seasonal time frame.

---

* *101 Quarterback Drills* by Steve Axman was published in 1998 by Coaches Choice Books, Champaign, IL; 1-800-327-5557.

DRILL PROGRESSION #1: WARM-UP THROW DRILL

Objective: To teach, coach and practice drop-back pass set-up and pass-delivery mechanics while warming all body parts for the actual passing/throwing motion, especially the passing arm.

Equipment Needed: One football; lined field.

Description: Two quarterbacks stand 10 yards apart working on a yard line. The passer stands on the balls of both feet. He checks for proper body stance: knees bent, football held up high near the throwing shoulder, back elbow up away from the body frame. The quarterback takes a proper pass-delivery step just outside of the yard line and executes a proper pass-delivery action of the football.

Coaching Points:

- The coach should check for proper carriage of the body and prepass-delivery stance.

- The quarterback steps beyond the yard line to properly open the hips for fluid pass-delivery action.

- The coach should emphasize bisecting the opposite quarterback, focusing on proper pass-delivery stepping and follow-through action of the body.

- As his arm warms up, the passing quarterback attempts to get horizontal accuracy by trying to hit the quarterback being thrown to "in the nose."

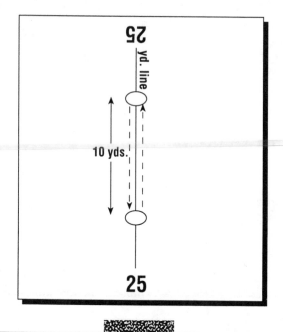

DRILL PROGRESSION #2: HIP WARM-UP THROW DRILL

Objective: To teach, coach and practice over-the-top pass-delivery mechanics of the upper torso while warming up and loosening the hips for the pass-delivery motion.

Equipment Needed: One football; lined field.

Description: Two quarterbacks stand eight to ten yards apart working on a yard line. The passers stand on the line with the balls of the feet both starting out with a 90° angle turn to the right. Without moving the feet, the quarterbacks open their upper torso to the left and execute a proper over-the-top delivery motion to the nose of the other quarterback. After sufficient repetitions, the action is repeated with the feet turned on a 90° angle to the left.

Coaching Points:

- No stepping action is involved in this drill. The feet face away from the line on a 90° angle to the left and right.

- The quarterback must be sure to raise the football above the shoulder in the pre-throw stance to execute a proper "over-the-top" pass delivery.

- Since no stepping action is involved, extra index finger follow-through to the opposite quarterback's nose should be emphasized.

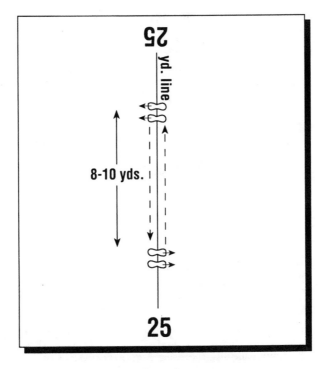

DRILL PROGRESSION #3: KNEELING THROW DRILL

Objective: To teach, coach and practice over-the-top pass-delivery mechanics of the upper torso while warming the upper-body torso, shoulders and passing arm.

Equipment Needed: One football; lined field.

Description: Two quarterbacks kneel with their left knee up (left foot just outside the line to ensure proper open hip action), seven to eight yards apart. The quarterbacks execute proper over-the-top pass-delivery action with proper index finger follow-through to the opposite quarterback's nose. After a sufficient number of repetitions, the quarterbacks switch to a double-knee kneel action and then to the right knee up.

Coaching Points:

- Through all three kneeling actions (left knee up, both knees down, right knee up), the passing quarterback must emphasize a proper high pre-pass hold of the football near the throwing shoulder.

- The variation of the knee positioning helps to vary the hold of the upper body torso during the various pass deliveries.

- Driving the ball with the chest should be emphasized.

- When both knees are down, the quarterback actually falls to the ground as he rolls into the throw with his belly and chest. The quarterbacks do not snap and break at the hips during this pass-delivery action.

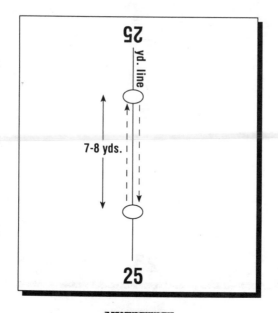

DRILL PROGRESSION #4: PRANCER THROW DRILL

Objective: To teach, coach and practice the "feel" of rolling the body over the ball of the front pass-delivery step while executing over-the-top pass-delivery mechanics.

Equipment Needed: One football; lined field.

Description: Two quarterbacks stand eight to ten yards apart on a yard line. The passer stands over the line with his forward pass-delivery step foot just beyond the line (to help properly open the hips for the pass delivery). The front leg is bent. The heel of the front foot is off the ground to help form the "prancer" stance. The quarterback executes his normal "over-the-top" pass-delivery action, emphasizing driving the ball with the chest and the rolling over the ball of the front foot.

Coaching Points:

- The quarterback should roll his body (especially his chest) over the ball of the front, pass-delivery step foot.

- The quarterback should be sure to execute a proper high hold of the football near the passing shoulder as he begins the rollover pass-delivery action.

- Proper index finger follow-through should be emphasized.

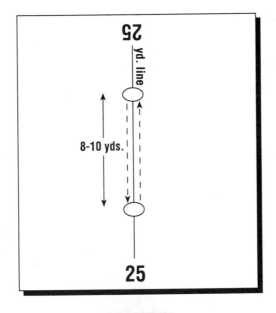

DRILL PROGRESSION #5: OFF BALANCE THROW DRILL

Objective: To teach, coach and practice the skills of proper over-the-top pass-delivery mechanics when not set properly due to pass rush.

Equipment Needed: One football per two quarterbacks.

Description: The quarterback is instructed, from a pre-snap stance with football in hand, to deliver a pass to the opposite quarterback off of the second or third step to the left and then to the right. The quarterbacks align seven to eight yards from one another.

Coaching Points:

- The quarterback should move away from his pre-snap stance as if under the center to the left or right and throw quickly from an unbalanced position off his second or third step.

- The quarterback, in an almost jump pass-type action, should get the football up into a high, near the throwing shoulder hold and execute a pass-delivery with extra index finger follow-through.

- The extra index finger follow-through and raised upper body torso separated from the off-balance lower run platform are critical.

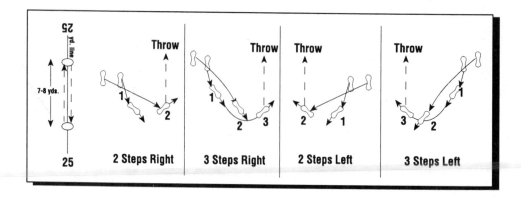

DRILL PROGRESSION #6: TRAJECTORY NET PASS DRILL

Objective: To teach, coach and practice high trajectory passes with the nose of the football turning over so that the football drops in nose-down.

Equipment Needed: 10-12 footballs; portable passing target net; lined field.

Description: Starting from an alignment twenty yards from a portable passing target net, the quarterbacks take their normal three-, five-, or seven-step drop (or whatever other drop action is used) and execute a high trajectory pass that drops nose-down into the passing target net. Left hash, right hash and middle of the field adjustments should be considered. After a desired number of passes from each hash and the middle of the field, the passing net is moved back five yards. The quarterbacks should practice such deep trajectory passes to both the left and the right.

Coaching Points:

- The quarterback should follow through to the zenith (highest) point of the pass with their lead step, chest and index finger follow-through.

- Proper follow-through to the zenith point of the pass allows the football to turn over and drop in to the receiver (target) nose down. Lack of follow-through to the zenith point of the pass will lead to a nose-up football which "dies" due to the fat of the football cutting through the air.

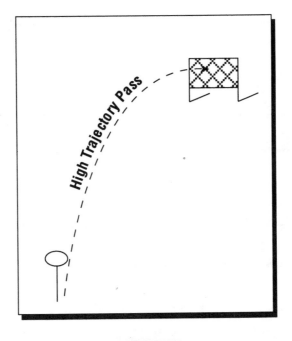

DRILL PROGRESSION #7: DOWN THE LINE MOVE PASS DRILL

Objective: To teach, coach and practice on-the-move passing mechanics.

Equipment Needed: One football per two quarterbacks; lined field.

Description: Two quarterbacks start on the sideline, each on a yard line 10 yards apart. The quarterback with the football jogs in place until the other quarterback runs out in front of him approximately five yards. At that point, the quarterback with the football runs forward and executes a pass on the run. When the opposite quarterback catches the pass he jogs in place until the other quarterback runs to a position five yards in front. That quarterback then begins running and executes an on-the-move pass. The repetitions are repeated all across the field.

Coaching Points:

- The coach should emphasize a high, near-the-shoulder carriage of the football, divorcing the upper-body passing action from the lower-body run action.

- Extra index finger follow-through should be emphasized to help fight the negative influence of the lower-body run action.

- The passing quarterback attempts to lead the other quarterback by a yard.

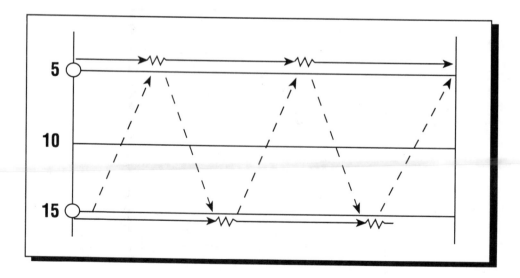

DRILL PROGRESSION #8: SET-UP DRILL

Objective: To teach, coach and practice the drop-back set-up actions that a particular offense may utilize.

Equipment Needed: One football per quarterback; lined field.

Description: Quarterbacks form a horizontal line along a yard line (to measure depth of drop). They take a pre-snap alignment, holding a football as if they were positioned to take a snap from the center. On one quarterback's cadence, they will all take the same, designated three-step, five-step, seven-step move, etc. drop-back action to the desired set-up launch point.

Coaching Points:

- The coach should check for proper depth and proper set-up action.

- It is important for the quarterback to have a proper, athletic carriage of the body in his pre-pass stance.

- On each repetition, the coach should tell the quarterbacks what set-up angle he wants (passing to the left/center/right) so the quarterbacks can practice such set-up actions.

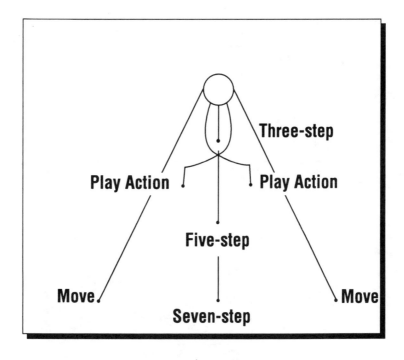

DRILL PROGRESSION #9: RE-SET DRILL

Objective: To teach, coach and practice re-set actions after the prime set-up to ensure athletic carriage of the body in the passing stance on a second, third, and fourth, possibly, re-set; to develop re-set athleticism and quick-footedness.

Equipment Needed: One football; lined field.

Description: Two quarterbacks align facing one another five yards apart. They toe the yard line to measure the depth of the drop. The coach stands in between the two quarterbacks. The quarterback with the football takes a three-, five-, or seven-step drop and sets up in a proper prepass-delivery stance. The coach then uses hand signals to either bail out set-up left or right, shuffle a yard or two left or right, act as if he's ducking under a jumping defensive lineman or step up into the pocket. The coach signals for three such re-sets. On the third re-set, the quarterback throws to the opposite quarterback. The exercise is then repeated by the other quarterback.

Coaching Points:

- Re-sets due to rush pressure are where quarterbacks often break down in their passing mechanics by resetting into improper prepass-delivery stances.

- The coach should check each re-set stance for proper knee bend, athletic carriage of the body and a high hold of the football in the vicinity of the back, throwing shoulder. The quarterback should not lock out his legs or hold the football at belt level.

- A right-handed quarterback bailing out to his left should bail-out with his back to the LOS to try to run over-the-top of a backside defensive end rush that he might not see.

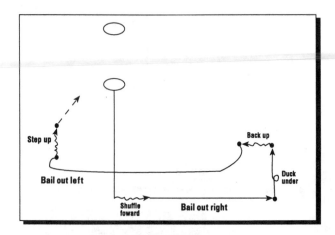

DRILL PROGRESSION #10: VARIED SET-UP AND THROW DRILL

Objective: To teach, coach and practice the various set-up skills of the Set-Up Drill that a particular offense may utilize and the passing mechanics of those set-up actions.

Equipment Needed: One football per two quarterbacks; lined field.

Description: This drill is the next step in the teaching progression of the coordinated pass drop and pass delivery for the variety of pass set-up actions that a particular offense will utilize. Two quarterbacks face one another, five to ten yards apart. On cadence, the quarterback with the football takes the determined drop (three-, five-, seven- step, straight drop back, move, play action, sprint-out, etc.). He delivers a pass to the opposite quarterback and then comes back to his original alignment. The other quarterback executes the drill in the same fashion.

Coaching Points:

- The quarterbacks should be told by the coach what type of pass delivery to execute. Is it five- to seven-step plant/throw (quick timing)? Is it five- or seven-step pop-up/throw (normal timing)? Is it five-or seven-step hitch-up/throw (delayed timing)? Five-step move action? Seven-step sprint-out?

- The coach should check for the integration of the varied set-up skills and subsequent pass-delivery skills utilized.

- On sprint-out, boot-leg and roll-out type set-up actions, the quarterbacks can initially align on one hash, execute their set-up action and throw to the other quarterback on the opposite hash. Each quarterback must be sure to get sufficient repetitions on the right and left hash to practice such set-up and throw actions both to the right and left.

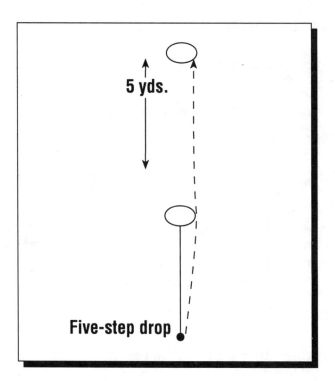

5 yds.

Five-step drop

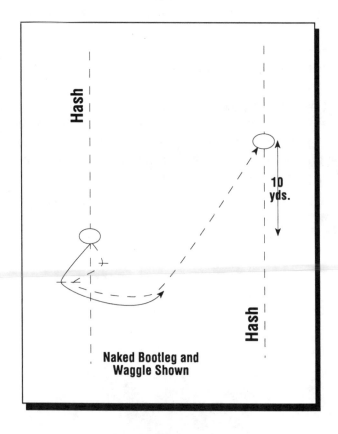

Hash

Hash

10 yds.

**Naked Bootleg and
Waggle Shown**

Steve Axman is the head football coach at Northern Arizona University. In his eight seasons at the helm of the NAU football program, Axman has led the Lumberjacks to national prominence. The 1996 season was highlighted by NAU's first-ever appearance in the Division I-AA postseason tournament. In addition, NAU became the first college team—at any level—to have both a 2,000-yard rusher (1996 Walter Payton Award winner Archie Amerson) and a 3,000-yard passer (Travis Brown) in a single season.

Prior to assuming his present position in 1990, Axman was on the coaching staff at the University of Maryland, where he coached the quarterbacks—most notably New York Jets signal caller Neil O'Donnell. Before his stint in Maryland, Axman served as the offensive coordinator at UCLA from 1987 to 1988. During his tenure on the Bruins' staff, Axman coached the quarterbacks—one of whom was NFL great Troy Aikman of the Dallas Cowboys. Axman has also coached pro quarterbacks Jeff Lewis (Denver Broncos) and Scott Zolak (New England Patriots). A 1969 graduate of C.W. Post College, Axman has also held positions on the gridiron staffs of Stanford University, the Denver Gold (USFL), the University of Arizona, the University of Illinois, the U.S. Military Academy, Albany State University, and East Stroudsburg State University.

A 29-year coaching veteran, Axman is widely renowned as having one of the most creative offensive minds in the game. An accomplished writer, he has authored several books and articles on football schemes, techniques and strategies, including the well received *Coaching Offensive Backs* (1998). Axman has also produced three highly successful instructional videos: *Coaching Offensive Backs*; *Winning Quarterback Drills*; and *Coaching Quarterback Passing Mechanics*.

Axman and his wife, Dr. Marie Axman, reside in Flagstaff, Arizona. They have four daughters—Mary Beth, Jaclyn, Melissa, and Kimberly.

ADDITIONAL FOOTBALL RESOURCES FROM

COACHES CHOICE

BOOKS:

■ *101 QUARTERBACK DRILLS*
by Steve Axman
1998 ▪ Paper ▪ 120 pp
ISBN 1-57167-195-1 ▪ $16.95

■ *COACHING OFFENSIVE BACKS (2nd Ed.)*
by Steve Axman
1997 ▪ Paper ▪ 216 pp
ISBN 1-57167-088-2 ▪ $19.95

VIDEOS:

■ *COACHING OFFENSIVE BACKS*
by Steve Axman
1997 ▪ Running Time: Approx. 48 min.
ISBN 1-57167-119-6 ▪ $40.00

■ *COACHING QUARTERBACK PASSING MECHANICS*
by Steve Axman
1998 ▪ Running Time: Approx. 41 min.
ISBN 1-57167-225-7 ▪ $40.00

■ *WINNING QUARTERBACK DRILLS*
by Steve Axman
1998 ▪ Running Time: Approx. 40 min.
ISBN 1-57167-226-5 ▪ $40.00

ADDITIONAL FOOTBALL RESOURCES FROM

COACHES CHOICE

■ ***THE DELAWARE WING-T: THE RUNNING GAME***
by Harold R. "Tubby" Raymond and Ted Kempski
1998 ▪ Paper ▪ 164 pp
ISBN 1-57167-166-8 ▪ $16.95

■ ***THE DELAWARE WING-T: THE PASSING GAME***
by Harold R. "Tubby" Raymond and Ted Kempski
1998 ▪ Paper ▪ 152 pp
ISBN 1-57167-165-x ▪ $16.95

■ ***THE DELAWARE WING-T: THE OPTION GAME***
by Harold R. "Tubby" Raymond and Ted Kempski
1998 ▪ Paper ▪ 156 pp
ISBN 1-57167-164-1 ▪ $16.95

■ ***101 DELAWARE WING-T PLAYS***
by Harold R. "Tubby" Raymond and Ted Kempski
1998 ▪ Paper ▪ 120 pp
ISBN 1-57167-163-3 ▪ $16.95

■ ***101 DELAWARE WING-T DRILLS***
by Harold R. "Tubby" Raymond and Ted Kempski
1998 ▪ Paper ▪ 116 pp
ISBN 1-57167-162-5 ▪ $16.95

TO PLACE YOUR ORDER:
U.S. customers call
TOLL FREE (800)327-5557,
or write
COACHES CHOICE Books, P.O. Box 647, Champaign, IL 61824-0647,
or FAX: (217) 359-5975

ADDITIONAL FOOTBALL RESOURCES FROM

COACHES CHOICE